Hidden
Angel

Tina Place

David Robert Tomkins-Place known to us all as **"Baby David"**

On the 23rd of February 2011 this little baby shocked us all by the sudden announcement that he was there. For eight months he had been developing in his mother's womb, no one knew this baby was there. As soon as David and Sophie learned of his existence they were thrown into the depths of despair, as they were told the devastating news that no heart beat could be found. Their lives and the lives of their families were about to change forever. Sophie and David at a young age of just 18 were about to endure a long hard emotional path, a path that would test their emotions to the limit. This book opens a window into not only their struggle with coping with a still born child, but also the effect it had on their family members. Whilst I acknowledge this book will be as hard to read as it was to write, I hope it will bring awareness to everyone who reads it. With up to 17 still births a day there will be many people who will be able to relate to Sophie and David's story and this is one of the reasons they have chosen to revisit one of the worst events of their lives.

The Author

This is her third book and although her first book was very hard to write over a period of time as it was a true story about her lovely granddaughter's difficult life, this book was even harder to write as it took everyone back through a devastating and emotional time that she would rather not revisit given the choice. Over the years she has experienced grief at all levels and when her beloved father died she felt like her world had been pulled away from beneath her, she experienced terrible deep grief that seemed to last forever. However, the grief she and everyone else felt for the loss of this beautiful baby was so much more intense and totally different to any other grief ever experienced.

Acknowledgements

THE PARENTS – David and Sophie. At such a young age they have both been through one of the most emotional and testing times of their lives. They have shown strength, courage and above all dignity throughout. Their love for one another has helped them to get through the terrible loss of their precious baby. My heartfelt thanks go out to them for opening up their hearts and re-living one of the worst times of their lives, to allow me to share with everyone their experiences as they struggle to carry on with their lives. The dignified way they have dealt with things have filled both sets of parents with deep pride.

THE GRANDPARENTS – Angie and Robert and of course my husband Dave. This was a situation that we as parents would hope we would never have to deal with. We felt our world crumble beneath our feet. As parents we want to protect our children and keep them safe from harm. Here we were thrown into a situation we had no control over. We could not take the pain away from our children this time. In a split second our youngest children had been thrown into parenthood and then cruelly had it ripped away from them. As grandparents we mourned the loss of our first grandson and even though our hearts were broken in two, we had to somehow find the strength to hold it together for our children's sake. Angie and Rob and my husband and I united together to support both our children as best we knew how.

THE GREAT GRANDPARENTS – Lillian, Ronald, Linda and Bob. They are loving, caring grandparents to Sophie and have taken David under their wings to give them as much support as possible.

THE UNCLES AND AUNTIES – Matt, Jim, Richard, Dean, Carl, Neil, Emma and Michaela. Their support was priceless to Sophie and David. When they first were told of the terrible news, they stopped in their tracks put everything to one side including their own feelings and rushed to the hospital to be at their youngest brother and sister's side.

THE COUSIN – Ella. To this day she keeps her cousins memory alive in her everyday innocent thoughts, words and actions. When we are at our lowest ebb, Ella seems to brighten up our thoughts by suddenly producing a picture that speaks a thousand words.

About this book

With the UK having one of the highest statistics for Stillborn babies this is a true story of two young people whose carefree lives were changed forever, when they were thrust into the realisation of becoming parents at a young age, without ever knowing there was a little baby growing inside its mother's womb. Within minutes of finding out this beautiful little baby boy existed he was snatched away from them, leaving behind total devastation for not only Sophie and David but that of their families. Sophie and David have opened up their hearts to allow this story to be written and allow everyone to experience the events that took place on the 23rd February 2011. We have all experienced pain and grief throughout our lives, but the grief that was encountered this day far exceeds any other grief ever experienced. It is something that will stay with everyone involved for the rest of their lives and no one will be able to get over the loss of our dear little hidden angel. We will however all have to learn over time to live with this loss. One thing is for sure and that is this little baby will never be forgotten. Although he never breathed our air, he certainly left his mark on each and every one of our hearts. We all have our individual memories and these we will remain with us forever.

Chapter 1

December 2010, Sophie had just had her 18th Birthday meal enjoyed with family and friends. She looked beautiful in her new size 12 blue dress, hair extensions and very high shoes. Just about everyone in the room had commented on how stunning she looked. Sophie had been suffering with a cold over the past month that just would not go away and had been washed out and looking pale for a long time. So it was good to see her looking so well. She had previously been to the doctors with an upset stomach and after an examination was told she was suffering from Irritable Bowel Syndrome and a note was made on her records that she was "NOT PREGNANT." All family members that came in contact with Sophie over the next few months grew increasingly concerned about her health. Sophie herself had put any fears of pregnancy behind her and also previous pregnancy tests showed a negative result. Her monthly periods were still happening every month although they were only lasting two to three days instead of her normal five day cycle. Throughout the year she had gone about life as any young person would, attending college along with David and enjoying camping holidays with friends. It was only the later part of the year that Sophie began to feel tired and lacked energy. She had been attending weight watchers and had been slowly losing weight.

Christmas and New Year were enjoyed in the usual way with Sophie and David sharing their time between both families. In January David's mum had sold her business and house and was looking forward to having a quiet few months. Sophie put her mark on David's bedroom in the new place by organising it her way. On the odd occasion both sets of parents would meet and David would either stay over at Sophie's house or Sophie would stay at David's. Tuesday evening David would always come home with his father after playing darts at the Pub his parents owned. On Tuesday evening of the 22nd February 2011 David participated in a darts match and at the end of the evening he returned home with his father. He had not seen much of Sophie this week as he had prior commitments with his Drama school. During the evening David had been texting Sophie and just before leaving the pub he would telephone her to say goodnight. Once at home just before going to sleep he would send his final text of the night to Sophie saying "goodnight Love you x." The next morning David asked if he could have a lift from his mother as she was on her way to a pamper morning. A usual Wednesday morning for Sophie started with her nana shouting good morning up the stairs to Sophie as she called in to pick the two retriever dogs up to take for a walk. Normally Sophie would always shout good morning back to her nana, but this morning she had been suffering with what she thought was bad period pains on and off and was trying to get some sleep. Angie, Sophie's mum had asked Sophie if she was okay before leaving for work, as she had seen her daughter going in and out of the toilet that morning. Sophie had explained she was just having bad period pains to her mum and that she would be ok. Sophie's first pain was just like a period pain and she had noticed traces of blood. Because she had been having regular monthly bleeds she just thought this was going to be a bad one. The pain got worse and travelled through to her back. It was now she began to feel very alone and frightened. The pain kept coming and going and to try to ease it Sophie lay as still as she could. She cried out loud but no one was about to hear her. She silently prayed David would come to her house soon. Angie had recently called Sophie as she had been worried about her. She told Sophie because it was half term she could just stay in bed and rest with a nice hot water bottle. Angie was under the same impression as Sophie and that was she was just having a bad period day. Convincing herself of this she carried on with her usual day at work. Eventually David arrived just before eleven o'clock. He found Sophie lying in her bed in a lot of pain. Nothing he seemed to do could make Sophie's pain any easier and so he eventually telephoned his mother for some advice. His mum at first thought Sophie may be suffering from a kidney infection, but after David's third telephone call to her, where he was crying uncontrollably he asked her to come quickly. She told him she would come straight away and to ring for an ambulance. Sophie's pains suddenly got much worse and became unbearable. She became very scared as she had never felt pains like this before. She felt an excruciating pain and ran to the bathroom where she collapsed on the floor as lots of water mixed with blood came away from her. Sophie felt like she was going to die and shouted for David, who at that time was still in her bedroom feeling very concerned and frightened for his girlfriend. She asked him to call an ambulance, which he had already done. Everything kept going black as she lay on the bathroom floor. She could see from David's face how frightened he was and his fear echoed in his voice as he kept telling her to stay awake. She had not been aware that she had been drifting in and out of consciousness and when David kept shouting at her to keep her awake her fear of feeling she was going to die only strengthened. She kept looking down at the amount of blood on the floor, whilst telling David over and over again she loved him just in case she died. Tina had already telephoned her husband Dave and told him to get the car ready as they needed to get to Sophie quickly and was on her way. Five minutes later they arrived outside of Sophie's parent's house. Tina ran straight up the stairs and was met by a panic stricken David. She pushed passed him to find Sophie on the

12

bathroom floor sitting in watery blood. The first thing she asked Sophie was 'could she be pregnant' as from experience she guessed her waters had broken or she was having a miscarriage. She turned to her son and asked him the same question, this time he told his mother he did not know and that they had had an accident back in June 2010, but had done several tests, which were negative. She cuddled her son as she found a towel to cover Sophie with. David's father had tried to come up the stairs, but had been stopped for obvious reasons and so he stood outside and waited for someone to tell him what was happening. David quickly called Sophie's Mum and told her what was going on. Obviously this shocked Angie as she had only spoken to Sophie a few hours earlier and although her pains had gotten worse, Angie had thought her daughter was just having bad Period pains which would eventually with rest would right itself. Angie immediately told her boss she needed to go to her daughter's side as she had been rushed into hospital. Her boss could see from the alarmed look on Angie's face how worried she was and tried to reassure her that Sophie was just probably panicking and would be alright. Angie then telephoned her husband Rob and insisted he made his way to the hospital as quickly as he could.

The paramedics finally arrived and the terrified look on David's face got worse. Sophie remembers this look haunting her. The paramedic kept asking her if she was pregnant, Sophie just kept looking up at David and kept saying over and over to him how sorry she was. She was confused, frightened and in a lot of pain and yet somehow she had to find the strength to throw some track suit bottoms on and walk down the stairs to the ambulance outside with the help of the paramedics. She was given gas and air and began to cry uncontrollably. David accompanied Sophie in the ambulance whilst his mother followed behind in his car. Dave returned to finish of his work at the pub. Tina managed to get to the hospital or so she thought before the ambulance and was met at the 'Accident & Emergency' department by Sophie's mum Angie. Angie had already been up to the reception area and they had told her Sophie had not arrived at that time. Her face spoke a thousand words. She had more or less convinced herself that Sophie was having a miscarriage. Angie had suffered a miscarriage when she was just 14 weeks pregnant with her third child and remembered it being one of the most painful experiences she had ever had. Angie was terrified of situations like this as a few years previous Sophie's parents had experienced one of their worst nightmares at that time, when their eldest son Jim had been taken to the 'Accident & Emergency department and Angie remembers not being able to find her son on arrival. It turned out her son was seriously ill and this obviously was a memory that still haunted Angie. Here she was again finding herself unable to locate her daughter, which brought back all the panic she had experienced on that occasion. Her eldest son Jim who was working with his father and brother Matt at the time had been frantically trying to contact Angie by phone, but Angie could not give them any answers to their questions as she did not know anything herself yet. She also rang her mother as she felt she needed to warn her too. Angie and Tina became like two women possessed as they frantically searched outside and inside for Sophie and David. They even had a member of the staff looking for them. Angie at this time had not realised that Tina had been in the house and seen the state Sophie had been in. It only came to light when Tina started to explain things a little bit more in depth to Angie. Tina rang her son's mobile but he did not answer, this caused more panic for both of them, but then David rang Angie's mobile asking where they were. He told her to make her way to the 'Maternity Unit' because that is where the ambulance had taken them. It had still not quite sunk in that Sophie must really be pregnant as she had never looked pregnant. The previous Saturday she had worn the same beautiful blue dress that she had worn on her 18th birthday party back in December. Angie and Tina drove round to where the 'Maternity Unit' was situated at the hospital. They were both still very confused by this, as they could not understand why they would take Sophie to a delivery suite if she was having a miscarriage. When they finally arrived at the reception area where Sophie and David were, Angie was quickly ushered to the delivery suite. Tina was told because she was not the mother of Sophie; she would have to wait in the reception area. Angie recalls thinking the room was very dark and still has problems to this day remembering everything about it. However, she remembers looking over at her daughter who was frantically drawing on the gas and air and the room being very hot. There seemed to be complete confusion and lots of people all talking at once. The midwives were trying to do an ultrasound scan but appeared to be having problems finding the baby. Angie felt frustrated at this point and remembers thinking if they could not find a baby, why was her little girl writhing about in pain. Sophie just kept looking at her mother and saying sorry for going to make her a Nan. Just a few minutes after Tina was left standing at the reception area in a total panic she saw her son David running up the corridor. He was pale and crying, he threw his wallet at his mother and asked her what he was going to do as he was going to be a dad and they did not have anything for the baby. He told her they were not ready for a baby as they did not know she was pregnant. She immediately told him to calm down and take a breath as at this moment in time he was not sure how far on Sophie was and also there were a lot of facts that needed to be sorted out first. So for the moment he just needed to take it one step at a time and no matter what happened both families would cope. He grabbed his mother's hand and told her both him and Sophie wanted her in the room.

Tina recalls that it was like a scene from 'casualty' when she entered the room. There were midwives and doctors everywhere. One doctor was attempting to locate the baby and she wondered immediately, as to why he was scanning at the side of Sophie, rather than on the front of her stomach. Sophie was clearly in a lot of pain, with Angie her mother sitting by her side with her head on the bed. The doctor began to speak as he moved up and down side to side with the scanner. Angie was as pale as the sheets on the bed. One of the nurses had given her a glass of water, as she felt like she was going to collapse. David was holding Sophie's hand tightly and stroking her hair at the same time. Tina had one hand on David's shoulder and one hand on Angie's shoulder. Everyone listened to what the doctor was saying. He looked closely at the scan and told them there was definitely a baby there. By this time we all could see that for ourselves, as we too could see a perfectly formed baby. He carried on telling everyone it was between 32- 35 weeks, good spine and a good size, but there was no heart beat it was 'dead'. Sophie only remembers little things about her arrival at the hospital. However no one in that room will forget the words of the doctor. She will never forget within a minute of being told she was going to be a mum, she was told her baby was dead. Angie could not comprehend that her size 12, 18 year old daughter could be pregnant to a baby that was not far off being full term, it was impossible. Angie recalls one minute being told she was going to be a grandmother and then having it snatched away from her so quickly. The midwife took hold of Sophie's hand and spoke gently to her, asking her if she understood what had just been said. The doctor made his way out of the delivery room leaving total devastation behind him. It was only at that moment realisation finally hit Sophie and everyone in the room. The doctor had actually been talking about her baby and not her. She wanted to scream out that they were so very wrong, but no words would come out of her mouth. Sophie answered immediately by repeating that her baby was dead. Grabbing for the gas and air she sucked as hard as her lungs allowed her to. The midwife then continued to explain that Sophie would still have to give birth to her baby and that meant she would have to do all the work, as with a live baby it would help mum to deliver it into this world. She felt numb as she looked around for David. Nothing seemed real, she felt she was having a nightmare and wanted to wake up from it. Her baby was dead and she had not known this baby was even there.

She felt hatred at herself and questioned why and how did she not know a baby was growing inside of her. By this time Angie, Tina, Sophie and David were in total meltdown and although the information was hard to take in, the bond they had all formed grew stronger by the minute, united in grief, holding onto each other and trying their best to try to hold each other up through this awful situation. Angie's heart was breaking at the thought of her little girl having to go through labour for nothing. She glanced up at David and recalled how pitiful the situation was for all concerned. The midwife asked Sophie in between labour pains if she wanted the baby to be placed on her chest when it was born. Sophie said she did not want this done. She was then asked if she would like to see the baby. Sophie did not stop to think about it and said they definitely did not want to see it. The midwife was very sensitive to this very upsetting situation. She continued to explain to Sophie and David that they would take the baby away and give them time to talk to each other and think about what they wanted to do. She told them there was no hurry to make any decisions and whatever they decided to do they would work round them to help them in any way they could. Whilst the midwife was talking to Sophie and David, Tina text her son Dean as he had text her asking what was happening. He knew Sophie had been rushed into hospital but that was all. How could you text such a horrible situation to someone, so all she sent was a message saying 'it is not good Dean, you may want to come up to support your youngest brother.' Dean remembers all too well receiving the text message from his mother and after reading it, he let his mind run a riot. The first thought that came to his mind was that Sophie was dying: A million and one things raced through his head all at once. Was it internal bleeding? Had something burst? Was she going to die? The hairs on his body were all standing up. Never could he have ever imagined what had really happened to them. All too soon it was time for the baby to be born. This was the time when everyone should have been excited; instead they were all trying their best to console each other. Sophie began to push and let out a long, loud screams which went on for what seemed like eternity. Tina looked down and there was a little baby's head. Her heart melted and her knees buckled. She had witnessed the birth of her first granddaughter and remembered the overwhelming feelings she had of pride and joy at watching her being delivered into this world and how she wished this could have been the same. Sophie gave one more push and little one was born. Both Angie and Tina could not believe how normal he looked. Their immediate thoughts were that the doctors and their machines had made a mistake and any minute now their little grandson would breathe and let out a cry. Both Angie and Tina felt like screaming as they both willed their little grandson to breathe, they have never prayed harder than they did at that moment, but the room remained silent. The silence was only broken when suddenly everyone started sobbing. Tina looked towards Sophie and David. Sophie just kept her eyes on David and did not dare to look anywhere else. The midwife cradled the baby who was wrapped in a towel in her arms. She broke the silence when she asked if they wanted to know the sex of their baby. Sophie and David both said yes together and so she peeled back the towel and told them their baby was a boy, before carrying his lifeless body out of the room, leaving behind sadness and tears instead of happiness and laughter. To be told you are going to be parents without knowing you were even pregnant and then for it to be snatched away in the blink of an eye, is something you read about in a book. You never imagine it to ever happen to you. Reality sunk in of the brutal decisions these two 18 year old kids would have to make; post mortems, funeral, whether to see their little boy. Tina and Angie consoled each other for a while just cuddling and holding the hands of their young children. Their path was going to be long and hard and they were going to need all the help and support they could get. Sophie had to have a few stitches after the birth of her son, so Angie and Tina went out into the corridor to make some phone calls, leaving David and Sophie to have a little bit of time on their own. Angie rang her husband Rob whilst Tina rang her husband Dave. Through the tears and sorrow the conversations were made as quietly as possible, because they were aware there were other mothers to be in rooms nearby waiting to give birth to their baby's. Angie went back into the room to sit with her daughter and David came out in the corridor with his mother for a breather. No words could comfort her frightened and devastated son, so they just stood together hugging each other. Tina kept telling her son she was so very sorry and only wished she could make things alright for them. Although she did not want to make things any harder for her son at this moment in time, she decided she needed to speak to him on his own about deciding whether or not to see his son. She told him she had never had the chance to see her baby and that has haunted her forever. She told him if they chose not to see him they would never be able to remember what he looked like and although it will be painful and upsetting they would remember him, remember his features and know who their son looked like. No matter how hard it may be they need to be able to remember him after all he was their first born no matter what. How cruel life suddenly felt as Tina thought about this little baby being Angie and Rob's first grandchild and hers and Dave's first grandson and yet he was not allowed to stay and be loved by everyone in the two families.

Dean remembers trying to find the exact ward from the vague directions that his mother had given him on the phone. Eventually after what seemed like a life time searching for the right ward, Dean telephoned his mother again for further directions. He never in a million years imagined it would be the maternity ward that he actually had to find. As Dean was standing at the reception desk with his daughter Ella at his side, he caught sight of his mother walking towards him and he could instantly see the pain etched all over her face. He remembers feeling devastated, confused and worried all at once. The receptionist had just explained to Dean that Ella could not be allowed into the ward as she was not Sophie's child. Tina, Dean and Ella went into the long empty corridor and sat on some seats located just outside the ward. Ella asked her nana why her face was so very red and why she was crying. She did not want to upset her by telling her the truth at that moment as it was too painful and Ella was only six years of age. Dean said he would take Ella over to his partner Michaela who was working in the hospital. Michaela was so surprised to see Dean and Ella at the reception where she worked and immediately guessed there was something wrong. Dean was trying to whisper to her what had happened, but there were a lot of people around and she did not quite understand the full extent of what he was trying to say. She grasped Sophie was in hospital and had just had a baby and Dean needed her to look after Ella, so he could return to David and Sophie and support them because something was wrong. Michaela therefore had to get permission to keep Ella with her. Dean promised to keep her updated as much as he could. At the time Michaela was about eighteen weeks pregnant and like everyone else she never knew Sophie was pregnant, it just seemed so unreal. Even when Dean eventually told Michaela that David and Sophie's baby was still born and also what they had named him, she still found it hard to accept. Michaela could not go up to the hospital to be with everyone and support David and Sophie, as she needed to look after Ella. Therefore she never got the chance to meet baby David and therefore this was one of the reasons she found it so hard to accept it had actually happened. She recalls it was like something she would read about in a magazine and never thought it would happen so close to home. Once Dean had returned to the ward Tina explained in more detail everything that had happened as they made their way to the family room where relatives could sit quietly and make cups of tea. When dean walked into the room he saw his youngest brother David sat there looking, pale, tired and completely drained. He felt like his heart was going to stop beating at that precise moment and everything seemed to be in slow motion. Dean walked over to David and hugged him tightly, whilst trying to fight back his own tears. He wondered if he was going to become an emotional wreck. Then he thought to himself, he was the older brother and so he knew he had to stay strong for David. He shrugged off his feelings and told David everything would be alright, even though deep down he knew this was going to be an incredibly difficult time for all concerned. Dean knows that out of everyone in the family David was the lively, bubbly one with not a care in the world type of person and this made Dean's heart break even more for him. Soon afterwards Sophie's dad Rob and brother's Matt and Jim arrived. As Angie was still sitting at her daughter's side, Tina explained as best she could to them what had happened. About half an hour later, Angie joined everyone leaving David and Sophie together to talk over what they wanted to do about seeing their son. It was a decision that could not be taken lightly. Both Tina and Angie hoped they would change their minds about seeing their son. They prayed they would be able to cope with holding their little boy for the short time they would be able to, before he would be taken away from them forever. David came into the family room to tell everyone that he and Sophie had decided to see the baby and that also they were going to have their son named and blessed and would like to have their family members with them for this. They too had decided they did not want their baby to have a post-mortem as this would be too much for them to cope with. Emma, David's eldest and only sister who lived in Newbury but worked in London, was travelling down to be at her brother's side. Richard was coming to the hospital with his dad. Carl, David's other brother was living in Newcastle and so could not be there. Sophie's brothers were already there with her dad. Sophie was moved into the room adjacent to the family room and the hospital chaplain came to talk with them first to explain everything to them. After about twenty minutes the chaplain left them alone to see their baby and told them she would come back when they were ready for her, but there was no rush, they could take as much time as they needed.

Baby David was brought into the private room where Sophie and David were waiting nervously for him, as both of them did not know what to expect. Sophie remembers her heart sinking as she looked for the first time at her beautiful baby boy. Once again she questioned herself as to how she could not have known he was there growing inside of her for all those weeks. As she cradled him in her arms for the first time, she could no longer contain her emotions and instantly the love that she felt for her son was unbearable for her to cope with. She knew her time with him would be short and precious as she had been robbed of all the pleasures a mother should get from her new born baby. She knew she had to make the most of the little time she had with him. As she looked down at her beautiful perfect little baby, she told him how she was devastated that she would never get to see him grow up and get to experience all the lovely cuddles and kisses that a mother should share with her baby. They spent a short while together before Sophie's family went in to see them. It was decided it would be too overwhelming for everyone to go into the room all at once, so as this was Angie and Rob's first grandchild it would be kinder to let them go in first. Angie's screams echoed through the corridors. She recalls she was overwhelmed when she walked into the room to see her little grandson by his beauty. He was gorgeous, so perfect. His skin was so soft and she absolutely loved him. No one in the family room said a word, they just all sat there with their heads down, only lifting them up briefly at hearing the sound of Angie's screams. Tina kept glancing over at Richard as he had been so very quiet and had not spoken since arriving in the room. He seemed to be struggling terribly with his emotions and wanted to be left alone quietly to try to deal with them in his own way. Emma was sitting next to Dean and they were quietly talking to each other. Dave and Tina sat on the window ledge together just holding hands. Angie was first to return to the family room. She made her way straight to Tina and threw her arms around her neck, telling her how beautiful and so very perfect he was. She just could not understand how and why this had happened. Full of apprehension and sadness Tina led her family through into the room where David was sitting holding his son in his arms on the bed next to Sophie. He was looking down at him and talking to him. It was at that moment Tina felt her heart burst. There was her baby boy now holding his own baby boy in his arms so tenderly at such a young age himself. She felt her breath get drawn from her body in one quick gasp and her head began to spin. It was all so very hard to cope with. David looked up at his family as they came into the room and his eyes pierced everyone's heart. First he glanced up at his father and then his eyes moved towards his mother as he held his tiny baby up for her to take him for a cuddle. As she cradled his lifeless body in her arms she could see exactly what Angie saw he was beautiful and just perfect, making it harder to understand why he did not survive. He looked very long in length and was wearing a cute little yellow and white striped outfit that the midwife had dressed him in. She carefully pulled him closer to her chest and again pleaded with god to let him take a breath. She softly whispered to him telling him he was her beautiful grandson, she would never get the chance to gaze into his eyes or feed and play with him, but no one would ever take the love she felt for him away from her memory. Tina believed deep down that her late father would protect and look after her grandson for David and Sophie until one day they could meet him again. She then kissed him and reluctantly passed him over to his granddad. As Dave glanced down at his little grandson's feet he looked over at Tina and whispered 'how big they looked, just like Dave's fathers feet had looked'. His eyes were full of tears and his mouth was quivering. He was desperately trying to control his feelings, but they were gradually breaking through bit by bit. Tina could barely see her grandson by this time let alone his feet, because of the ocean of tears she had in her eyes. Dean looked over at Sophie; he remembers feeling like he just wanted to curl up in a ball and die when he saw her. He felt he could hardly look her in the eyes as she looked so young and frightened and her grief was plain for all to see. He went over to her and hugged and kissed her for the first time ever. He had already been struggling not to break down as he followed his family into the room, but as he caught sight of his beautiful nephew, newborn and so innocent, who had never been given a chance, he felt a tear run down his face. It was no good he had tried to hold it together for David and Sophie's sake, but like everyone else in the room he crumbled at this point. He felt like he had been stabbed through the heart. Every member of the family that wanted to hold baby David did, before returning to the family room to take time out to gather their thoughts. Sophie's heart and arms ached for her baby when other members of the family were holding him, but she unselfishly just sat back and watched firstly her family and then David's family cradle him carefully and lovingly in their arms. David and Sophie were then left alone for a short while again until the chaplain from the hospital arrived back. She spent a few brief moments with them to calm both their emotions down before the blessing.

The door to the family room squeaked open; no one had noticed the squeak before now. Everyone had been sitting silently gathering their own individual thoughts until the noise from the door interrupted them. The midwife invited them all to return to David and Sophie for the blessing. First, Angie walked in followed by Tina, then Dave, Rob, Matt, Jim, Dean and Emma. Richard reluctantly walked in last. He had not wanted to go in the first time as he found it too distressing and he most certainly did not want to see his young brother so upset again for a second time. None of us wanted to see one of our youngest family members have to go through such a traumatic event, but all our feelings had to be pushed to one side for now to be strong for David and Sophie. As we walked into the room we saw David sitting near the top of the bed holding tightly onto Sophie and baby David was now laid in the cradle which was placed in the middle of the bed. He had a blue and white blanket which had been carefully placed over him, with his little arms resting over the top of it. Sophie and David knew instantly that the name they had chosen for their son was right. Both the granddads were strong men who took their roles as head of the families very seriously and so they wanted their baby to have both their names and bring them together as one in name. David after his paternal granddad and father, Robert after his maternal granddad, Tomkins, Sophie's surname and Place, David's surname. The hardest thing was saying his name to everyone. Sophie was unable to get the name out when it came to her telling her family and needed David to help. She did not want to admit her beautiful baby boy would never use his name and that all it would become is a name on a page in the book of remembrance. Sophie admitted she is not religious, but by having the blessing she would like to think it helped her little boy become her beautiful little angel. When she looked around the room at everyone and saw how they were all absolutely distraught and weeping continuously, she realised the full extent of devastation today's events had brought upon them. She told herself at least her little baby had not suffered and that had to stand for something.

Eventually the chaplain began by thanking everyone for being there to support David and Sophie through their sad occasion as she handed out specially prepared sheets for baby David's blessing. She could see how strong and united both sets of families were and this brought joy to her heart as she knew they would get so much love and comfort from them. Everyone tried their hardest to join in the service, but by this time everyone was feeling like they were going to have to be scraped of the floor by the end of it. Not one person had managed to keep their feelings in and nobody cared who saw them cry. The blessing was a nice way for everyone to say their goodbyes, but it finally broke us all, even the strongest amongst us. Dean remembers looking around at everyone crying and confirmed it was one of the worst things he has ever had to do. He kept telling himself nobody should go through this, especially not his little brother. Although baby David looked perfect and looked like he was just sleeping peacefully everyone knew the truth and it just did not seem fair. This was a sleep this baby would never wake from. We all had been robbed from ever being able to hear him cry, hear his first words being spoken or seeing his first smile, or helping him with his first steps. Life was never going to be the same ever again for David or Sophie or any of their family members, there would always be something that would suddenly remind us when we least expect it, of our little sleeping angel. Soon the service was over and we were all left again in the room with David and Sophie all holding onto the service sheet and pretending to read it over again, or just do something to take our minds off the sadness of the situation. After a phew minutes we all began to talk to each other as we glanced several times at little baby David lying in his cradle. Every emotion that had ever been thrown at someone was being displayed in the room at that moment, anger, frustration and sadness. We knew it was going to be a long hard struggle to begin to feel like smiling again, this day would stay with us all forever. After about twenty minutes Tina told David and Sophie she was going to leave them to have some precious time with their lovely son, even though she wanted desperately to remain there for as long as she could, because she knew when she walked out of that room, it would be the last time she would ever see her grandson. She bent over the cradle and kissed her grandson ever so gently on his little cold soft face, before walking away from him forever. Even though only a few short hours had passed since he was born Tina noticed some changes in his colouring around his little ears and this brought the reality of his death back to her. This had to be one of the hardest things she had ever had to do in her life, leave her youngest son and his beautiful partner, whom she had become very close to and fond of with the pain they had to deal with, and having to leave behind her lovely grandson knowing she will never see him again. Emma took a photograph for everyone to have as a memory of him and once she had done this everyone seemed to want to have a photograph on their phones of him. Then one by one everyone left the room, their heads bowed down, eyes filled with tears and tongues silent. Sophie told David by having all the family present at the blessing made her realise their son was being acknowledged as part of the family and everyone will take away their own memories of him.

The next morning Tina received a call early from Angie asking her to come to the hospital and support her, as David and Sophie had decided they wanted to see Baby David for one last time. Tina was horrified at the thought of them doing this as she knew baby David's appearance would have changed dramatically since last night. She drove to the hospital and stood at the side of Sophie and David. She told them that they had both shared their precious time with their baby last night and should probably leave it at that. Last night whilst in their arms he was their lovely little baby boy, but this morning he would not look anything like that and today as harsh as it sounds, he would look like a 'dead baby' and this would be their last image of him. David stopped his mother in her tracks and told her that they too had noticed a change in their son during the time they spent with him and therefore had decided not to see him again. They had been told they could have their baby son with them all night if they wanted to, but as hard as it was for them to part with him, they chose to do it after a few hours because of the changes to his little body. Both mothers' were relieved to hear that they were not going to see baby David again. They both knew that if they had gone through with it, not only would it have been a shock to them but also that afternoon they would have wanted another glimpse of him and then maybes another tomorrow and where would it stop, after all it is only human nature for parents to want to see their new baby over and over again. Shortly after Tina arrived Angie had to leave for work as she could not get the time off work, because no one else could do her job. Tina promised she would be there all day. About an hour after Tina arrived, the door opened and in came Dean with a carrier bag full of goodies to eat. He had a tin of biscuits and some chocolate mini muffins. He made everyone laugh by telling them he had brought them as they had to be eaten because they had been lying around for a while. Dean said he was prepared to do anything at that time to steal a smile from David and Sophie and was prepared to stay at the hospital as long as he could to support them. The muffins were like glue and the biscuits were quite soft but it certainly lightened the sombre moment. He tried his utmost to cheer David and Sophie up and stop their minds from wondering back over the past 24 hours. David would be messing about one minute, making us all laugh and then in an instant his mood would change. It was such a tense day for us all and it was about to get harder for Sophie and David as they were waiting to get the all clear to leave the hospital.

The nurses kept coming in and out of the room and eventually the doctor came to check Sophie over, once he was happy she was ok he told her she could go home. The midwife who had been taking care of them brought a beautiful box in and gave it them before they left. The box had carefully selected items placed in it and that was all that Sophie and David were carrying out of the hospital. They both struggled to walk through the revolving doors at the hospital, knowing their beautiful baby was staying there without them. Sophie found this unbearable. All the time she had been at the hospital she was close to her baby and even though she had made the decision not to see him again she still knew that whilst she was in the hospital she could change her mind. Sophie felt she was walking away from her baby, leaving him all alone in the mortuary and hated herself for it with every step she took. They both had said their goodbyes, given him as many kisses and cuddles as they could and now on leaving the hospital they realised it was final. Sophie broke her heart in the car on her way home and David tried his hardest to offer her some comfort. To make things worse for Sophie her milk had now started to come in, just another reminder that her body had just gone though all the trauma of giving birth and she had nothing to show for it apart from the tiny memory box which she was holding tightly in her hands. Sophie's mum tried her level best to help her daughter, but was struggling with her own feelings from the loss of her grandson. Tina found it very hard to go up the stairs to the bathroom at Angie's house where she had last seen Sophie on the floor, as the memory was still so very fresh in her mind.

A couple of days after getting out of hospital Sophie decided to go and stay at David's parents place as it was by the sea and very peaceful. David and his family had only been there a few weeks and because it was in a secluded quiet location she would not get disturbed. Sophie's milk coming in was causing her a great deal of pain, so Angie and Tina used a method that had been given to them years ago and used a big scarf to bound her breasts up, to give her some support and relieve her discomfort. It did not look elegant but it certainly worked for Sophie. The health visitor came to see Sophie whilst she was there and had a nice chat with her about what had happened and what they felt may have caused her baby to be still born. She was given a telephone number to call if she needed anything and was told they would keep a check daily on her blood pressure until it was back to normal. Sophie's blood pressure had been very high whilst in the hospital on and off and was still not back to normal yet. They said they would come to her as it would not be fair for her to go to the clinic where people visit with their new born babies. Although still struggling with coming to terms with their loss, they still had to visit a funeral parlour and arrange a funeral for their little baby. They had decided to use a friend's funeral called 'Searsons family funeral.' David had attended college with Matt their son and trusted them. The owners Andy and Debbie had gone through having a still born baby girl some 5 years earlier and therefore knew exactly how they were feeling. Andy and Debbie were able to sit down and talk through everything they needed to arrange with Sophie, David, Angie and Tina. They were given some advice on what kind of things needed to be included in the service. Then they were told to go away and have some thoughts on what they would like for the songs etc. A date was set for the funeral, 11th march 2011. Everyone waited eagerly to hear that baby David had been taken out of the hospital mortuary and brought to the funeral parlour. It was something that gave all family members peace of mind as no one wanted him to be left in the mortuary. It affected Sophie badly and her sleep pattern was all over the place. David was supporting Sophie so much that he was neglecting himself and they had not spent one night apart since the death of their baby. David had dark rings under his eyes and his mum became increasingly worried about his own state of mind. It had brought back memories for his mum and dad of when they had lost their last child 14 years previous and he was aware of the affect it was having on them. Tina was trying to support them both as best she could and was driving them everywhere to take away any unnecessary pressures from them. An appointment had been made to register the birth and death of their baby and once again it was another event that was going to be hard for Sophie and David to deal with, but it was something that had to be done. They had made one of the first appointments just in case there were other births being registered that day. As soon as Sophie, David and Tina arrived, they were taken straight in to the private room. The lady that dealt with them was very sensitive to the situation and without rushing them she managed to get the birth and death certificate issued as quickly as she could. She explained because their baby did not take a breath she could not issue a birth certificate and death certificate separately. So a certificate of 'still birth' was issued. It seemed they would never get away from the word 'Still birth'. After getting the certificate they immediately took it to Andy at Searsons Family Funeral parlour so he could get baby David from the mortuary at the hospital.

The next day Sophie needed to be checked and the midwife had asked her to go to the clinic. Sophie eyes were the size of saucers as she knew she would have to walk empty handed into a clinic where all other mothers would be arriving for their checkups with their bundles of joy. Sophie raised the question with the midwife and she assured her that she would be taken into a separate room as soon as she arrived at the clinic. Tina Drove Sophie and David to the clinic for the appointment at 11.30 a.m. Sophie pressed the button on the wall and told the receptionist who she was and the time of her appointment. There were two other people in the waiting room with their new born babies. Tina watched Sophie very closely and held back her own feelings as she watched the new mothers fussing over their babies. Each minute felt like an hour. Another mother and baby came in and then another. Tina got up and told Sophie and David she could not take any more and was going to wait in the car. At twelve o'clock David text his mother to say they were still in the waiting room. Tina got out of the car and pressed the bell on the wall. She angrily explained to the receptionist that it was absolutely disgusting that a young couple who had not even buried their son had to be in the same room as the other mothers with their babies. She told Tina that they had gone in to see the midwife and apologised as they were not aware Sophie had turned up for her appointment. This had been a very upsetting situation for Sophie and David. It was a situation that should not have happened, but this would be one of many painful situations that they would have to endure in their everyday lives.

Dean and Michaela had kept very quiet about her twenty week scan which was now due. Michaela had invited her mum to the twelve week scan and so she had invited Tina to this one a while back. However after seeing baby David on the scan in the hospital, Tina could not bring herself to go to another scan so soon after that one. She felt that she would spoil the moment for Dean and Michaela and in her heart of hearts she knew they wanted to have a boy and they were going to ask the nurse to tell them at this scan. Tina secretly hoped that they would not be having a boy and felt really bad for thinking that. Therefore when Michaela asked her again if she would come, Tina declined even though she felt very sad at not being able to be with them for this lovely exciting occasion and she felt she was letting them down, but it was just too overwhelming for her. Dean tells of how both Michaela and he did not want to mention the scan in front of anyone because of the circumstances. They both wanted a boy and now they felt this would be rubbing salt in the wounds. Once Dean got into the scan room, he silently hoped that it would be a girl now. When the nurse told them they were having a boy, Dean took a deep breath. Part of him was pleased as this is exactly what he wanted and part of him was shattered, as he now knew he would have to try and find a good way of telling Sophie and David. Michaela was overjoyed that their baby was going to be a boy but she too had mixed feelings about how to tell David and Sophie. She realised it was going to be very upsetting for them both and gave lots of thought to how she was going to tell them and other family members. She felt the best way for her to do it was to put it on facebook. Sophie was one of the first people to leave a congratulations comment and when Michaela read it she felt full of guilt. It was never going to be easy for any of them but again it was another situation that had to be faced.

David and Sophie had been by each other's side every minute since the death of their baby son. Family members had said this traumatic experience would draw them closer together or push them further apart. It had brought them ever closer together. They were spending much of their days trying to sort out funeral arrangements and had popped back to see Andy about the songs they had chosen. They had hoped their son would have been collected from the hospital mortuary by now and was upset to find out that he was still there on his own. Andy showed Sophie, David, Angie and Tina a few ideas for a casket for baby David. Tina had decided she really did not want to look at them. She remembered attending her friend's baby funeral years ago and she never forgot how she felt seeing the small white casket. It was one of those occasions that you hope you will never have to deal with. Once back at home everyone got on with trying to decide what they wanted to say at the service. Carl had sent a poem that he had written for baby David and Sophie and David had decided to include it into the service. They did not want to make the service religious because of the way they were feeling. Finally Andy let Sophie and David know he had picked up their son from the hospital and it lifted their mood immensely, so Tina decided to take them to town to try and find something to wear for the funeral and also to pick up some little bits for baby David. After walking around the shops for what seemed like ages they could not find anything to wear for the funeral, so they went into the shop they had left till last. Sophie and David wanted to pick up a teddy to put into the casket with their son and a blanket to cover him. Sophie and David went together to one end of the shop leaving Tina to go on her own to pick a cardigan for him. She wanted to get one because every time she thought of her grandson she could picture him in the yellow striped suit with short sleeves, leaving his little arms exposed. They met back up at the checkout and strangely Sophie and David had picked up a blanket that matched the cardigan that Tina had picked up. The teddy bear was beige in colour with a little blue top and written on it was 'My First' Sophie cradled it in her arms tightly and kept stroking its ear. They made their way straight to the funeral parlour to give them to Debbie. Debbie asked if they would want to see their son at any time, but they told her they wanted to remember him the way he was on the day he was born. She asked Tina if she wanted to put the cardigan on baby David and because she is hard of hearing said yes to Debbie. It was only because of the look on David and Sophie's face that she realised she had said something wrong. David told her what Debbie had asked and she immediately said she would leave them to do it for her. Whilst there David handed over the design and words he wanted on the casket together with something that Angie had written from both families. A few items were given to them for the casket. Ella, baby David's cousin had given them a necklace made out of pasta and lovingly painted with a handmade card. Angie had given them a teddy that had belonged to her years ago when she was young, but had been shredded into bits by a pet dog. Tina gave them a letter and David gave them his guardian angel stone together with a letter from him and Sophie. However, the teddy that they had chosen to go in with baby David was still being held onto tightly by Sophie she just could not let it go and so a different smaller teddy was put into the casket in its place. The arrangements for his funeral had taken time and patience; it was lovingly put together in small stages. The support they were receiving was second to none but no one could take away their pain. Everyone chose to get their own flowers and when it came down to ordering them both sets of grandparents went together with Sophie and David. Angie and Rob picked out a heart cushion from them and their sons' Jim and Matt, Tina and Dave picked out an open ended spray, Emma, Neil, Richard, Dean, Michaela, Carl and Rachel picked out a teddy bear with white flowers and a blue ribbon. and Sophie and David picked out the letters' SON' in white flowers with baby blue ribbon and yellow roses in the middle of each letter. Once the flowers had been chosen Angie, Tina, Sophie and David went to see the final design for the casket which Andy had on his lap top, together with the final leaflet for the service. We left the funeral parlour in pieces and knew that the actual day was going to tear our hearts out. It was now the day before the funeral and the last pieces had to be tied up. Angie had received her 150 blue balloons off the internet. Dave and Tina went to a shop to pick up the gas to blow them up. Andy came to Tina and Dave's lodge which is by the sea and where Sophie and David had both decided this was the place they wanted baby David to make his final journey from. Andy always likes to plan the route out and check the times to ensure everything was in order to guarantee the funeral went smoothly on the day. It seemed like there was so much still to organise and the whole day was taken up between families putting the final pieces together. That evening was spent making sure both Sophie and David had everything they needed and giving them as much support as possible. Both families had come together to offer their support and uncles and aunts from Sophie's family who lived outside of Portsmouth had already arrived down to be by her side.

Chapter 2
David tells the story in his own words.

David had struggled so much with everything that had happened. He had never spoken much about the events that unfolded on Wednesday 23rd February 2011, until he was asked to describe in his own words how he felt for this book. He sat down quietly to think about what he wanted to say and began to write his own version of events for the first time ever. This chapter is written from his heart.

I can still remember that day like it was yesterday. I was helping out at the Drama school I attended for the past few days. We had decided because it was half term that we would clean out the costume and props room. This is a massive job so I knew it would take up most of my time over the half term. Sophie was not very happy about this, as obviously she wanted to see me at some point. I had already worked on the Monday and Tuesday but as I had been giving a shift to work at my parent's pub on the Wednesday evening, I had decided not to help out this Wednesday at drama. This would mean I could also spend some time with Sophie. As I had a dart match on the Tuesday night I returned home with my father because I am always a bit worse for wear afterwards. I woke up at around 10 o'clock and had a feeling that I needed to call an ambulance. I could only put this feeling down to a dream. It took me nearly an hour to sort myself out. I had spoken to Sophie in the morning just after I had woken up and knew that she wasn't feeling too well, so I decided to go this morning and see her instead of waiting till after dinner. When I arrived at her house she was still in bed so I snuggled up next to her and we started chatting about the usual rubbish that couples talk about. Her pains in her lower back were starting to get worse, so I rang my mum and asked her what she thought it might be. From what I described to mum she thought it may have been the start of a water infection, so I phoned Sophie's doctors surgery and tried to make an appointment. As it was short notice I could not get one, but the surgery has a walk in centre that is open from 3 o'clock, so I got Sophie some pain killers and a hot water bottle and we were just going to relax until it was time for the appointment. About 10 minutes later would be the start of the worst moments of my life. All of a sudden Sophie jumped out of bed and ran to the toilet. As I watched her I could see fluid coming out of her. My first reaction was that she had wet herself, which I thought would be natural if she had a water infection, but underneath I just had a horrible feeling. About 5 minutes past and sill I had not heard anything from Sophie, so I thought that she might be cleaning herself up. Suddenly I heard a faint call of my name from Sophie. I went to the bathroom door but did not go in and that is when she said "I think my waters have broken." I thought what the hell is she going on about. I remember asking her why she thought that, to which she replied in a rather loud voice "because I've wet myself." Then there was an almighty scream from her and it was then I started to realise something was so terribly wrong. So I grabbed my phone from the bedroom and where I was panicking so much I couldn't unlock it. When I finally calmed myself down I rang my mother again, as soon as I heard her voice I began to panic again and started to cry. I told my mother I thought Sophie was going to die and she told me she would come straight over and to call an ambulance straight away. I hung up and phoned 999. I explained to the operator what was happening, he asked lots of questions, where we lived? How old Sophie was, etc. I just remember thinking I don't care about all that just get me an ambulance. Sophie was sat on the toilet and the operator kept telling me she has all the signs of being in labour. I just kept thinking is everyone stupid, there was no way she could be pregnant, as we always used protection. But coming to my senses, I had to get Sophie of the toilet as it would be dangerous if she gave birth whilst sitting on it. So she slid down to the floor and was leaning against the bath. The operator then told me that the ambulance was there and I had to get any animals in the house and lock them in a room. Well Sophie has two dogs and two cats. I explained to Sophie that I had to go and put the

48

animals away, she kept saying "pleases don't leave me" and constantly saying "I'm sorry." I felt like a mad man running around the house looking for the dogs. Then I remembered that Lil Sophie's Nan takes them out for a walk on a Wednesday. I found the cats in the front room so I just shut the door. I was also told I had to keep the front door open, so I opened that before running back upstairs to Sophie. I heard a voice from downstairs, I thought it was the ambulance so I popped my head over the banister and it was just some random woman holding a parcel. She said that the parcel she had in her hands had been dropped at her house. I just snatched it out of her hands and ran back upstairs, thinking about it now she must have thought I was the rudest person she had ever met. Twenty minutes had past now and I was shaking so much, Sophie was losing so much blood now and I remember holding her hand whilst looking at this pool of blood on the floor. She went as white as a sheet and was slowly losing grip of my hand. I just kept saying to her "don't you dare stop breathing on me. Keep talking to me." She just kept saying over and over again "I'm so sorry David. How can I be pregnant?"

This is when mum came in with dad, I was so nervous. I had no idea how they would react but I think like me they were in shock. Mum went straight past me to Sophie and was trying to make her more comfortable; I went into the bedroom and burst into tears again. I just could not handle seeing Sophie in the state she was in. I just kept thinking I wouldn't know what to do if she died on me. Then the ambulance finally turned up after going to the wrong street and they told us that she was definitely in labour. They brought the gas and air out to give to Sophie to help her with her pain. Mum came into the room with me and asked me if I knew she was pregnant. I told her she had not told me if she was. This was when mum said that she thought Sophie may have had a miscarriage. I then had to call Sophie's mum Angie and tell her that Sophie was being rushed into hospital and that she needed to meet us there. Mum made me find something for Sophie to wear and then I followed the paramedics downstairs, stopping every now and then for Sophie. Once we were both in the ambulance and settled they took us to the hospital. On the way I remember the ambulance man asking me if we knew she was pregnant and me telling him we did not know. He then just said "congratulations." I felt my stomach turn. I remember thinking how am I going to be able to provide for this child, I have no job. I am over half way through a college course we both still live at home, all thoughts like this running around in my head. I just couldn't come to terms with any of it. I remember thinking is this a practical joke. When we finally arrived at the hospital we were taken straight to the maternity unit. I was just looking around and thinking to myself what am I doing here and at one point I was miles behind Sophie. The ambulance women had to wait behind for me. I just went into a complete daze. Then I saw Sophie turn around and hold her hand out for me, this made me snap out of it and I held her hand as tight as I could. They took us straight into a delivery room and the next time I looked up we were surrounded by midwifes, one came to me and held my hand and explained what they were about to do to Sophie. Sophie was now out of it on gas and air. I rang Angie again to see where she was and she told me that she was at the Accident and Emergency department. I told her where Sophie and I were and waited for her and mum to arrive. Angie and mum had met up and so they rushed to the maternity unit. They started scanning Sophie and I remember just looking at the screen and seeing this figure of a baby and my heart just melted. All the worry had gone because I knew that what I was seeing was my baby. By this time Angie had entered the room but my mum was not there. Angie told me that they would not let her in because she was not family of the mother. I decided to go and get her because I knew they would not stop me taking her in and I needed my mother with me. I ran up the corridor to find her and as I saw her I just blew up and started saying 'after she gives birth you need to go and get clothes and beds and everything mum', I remember her just taking my hand and gently saying to me "Ok David let us just get this out the way first, you don't know how far on she is or anything yet." So we went into the room. As we arrived there was a doctor there just starting to do another scan. I could not understand why they were doing this. The baby was round near Sophie's side and back and not in the front as it should be. Then a doctor who was looking at the scan just said he thinks the baby is about 32- 35 weeks, good size, good spine but no heartbeat, dead. My whole world crashed in an instant. Sophie let out a sound that pierced straight through my heart, all I can remember doing is gripping her hand and kissing her head. The midwife explained things gently again to Sophie and then she let out another almighty scream and two seconds later I saw the baby. Shortly after the midwife asked us if we wanted to know what sex the baby was. When we answered her she told us we had had a boy and then he was gone within a split second. I remember just standing there with my hands on my head saying "I don't know how this has happened" once everything had calmed down a little, the midwife who had never left our side, which was the most comforting thing she could do for us, started to explained everything and just talked about random things and it really helped. Then Sophie had to be sorted out after giving birth so I left her and her mum to sort that out whilst I went for a little walk with my mother to try and clear my head as it was spinning. She calmly tried to get me to think about seeing my son at some stage, as she never got the chance to see her baby, she did not want Sophie and I to never know what our baby looked like. Then mum and I went into a room that the hospital gave us for the family to sit quietly. I had heard that my brother Dean, Sophie's Dad Rob and two Brothers Jim and Matt were here too, I was nervous because I did not know how they would react as I felt that they were entitled to knock my head off as I had brought so much pain to Rob's baby girl and Jim and Matt's baby sister. As I was walking through the maternity unit I had no idea where I was going, I was just walking then I saw Jim and I remember him just coming up to me saying that he was sorry and giving me a hug, it was then that I realised I had nothing to worry about that I was just being silly. I remember walking into the room and everyone coming up to me giving me hugs and saying that they were so sorry, but I just felt like I was the one that should be apologising to them. I just kept blaming myself in my head and I wanted the midwife just to come into the room holding my baby and him to have started to breathe, but I knew that that would never happen. I was in the room for what felt like ages, it was weird because we would be completely silent one minute then the next we all would be laughing about something stupid then go back to being upset because we remembered what had just happened. I remember at one point I was just walking up and down the room to see how wide it was, then I realised that I needed to tell people in the family, but I just could not talk to anyone. That is why I needed Dean there because I knew that he would be able to hold it together for me, and also I had mum there to ring people. As I was due to work the pub dad had to work my shift. Once Sophie had had a shower I went back in to see her. When I walked in she was sat eating some toast and having a cup of tea with Angie. I'm the sort of person that is always happy and always wanting to make people laugh or if they are feeling down or upset, then I am the one who will try and make them feel better, but this time it's me that is feeling like this and I cannot help but shut myself off from this feeling. So the first thing that came into my head was to make Sophie laugh, so I made a joke about her eating my toast and drinking my tea and something about a hotel, the joke was terrible but we were in such a whirlwind of emotions that we found ourselves laughing uncontrollably, then I just gave her the biggest hug and kiss that I have ever given anyone and it was at that moment that I knew health wise she was going to be alright and that gave me comfort. I knew that my job now was to look after her and nothing else mattered.

We then got moved into another private room, this was nice because we could try and relax and the whole family could be with us. The midwife asked us if we would like to see baby and without any hesitation we said "yes." A service that the hospital offer, is they have a Chaplain who can give a blessing to our baby, we thought this was a good idea but we wanted to have both families there, so we told the midwife and she said that would be fine and to just let them know when they are going to all be there and then they can give us a time. Dean had phoned my sister Emma who lives in Newbury, but works in London and she left work straight away and headed down. We had to wait for my Dad to find a replacement to work my shift; he was going to give my other brother Richard a lift up with him. Unfortunately, my brother Carl lived in Newcastle so he could not get down that evening but I had spoke to him on the Phone. It was now late evening, Emma had arrived safely, and all the emotions came out when she cuddled me. I have no idea why but I have such a close bond with my sister. Mum received a phone call from dad saying that they were outside and that they were not allowed in, so I went outside to the reception desk. Dad just walked straight up to me and gave me a hug. I could see that he was struggling to keep his feelings in, he has always been the strong one and I don't think that I have ever seen him cry up until this point. Even so he was still managing to hold it together and I took a lot of strength from him in that moment. I remember just thinking that now it's my turn to grow up and become the man he is, because I have my own family now and have a long hard struggle ahead of me and I have to be that pillar of strength like he is for my girlfriend and family. Then Rich gave me a massive hug and did not let go until we got to the room. We were all sitting in the room talking and my head started to feel like it was going to explode. I've never felt pain like it I looked up and everything was starting to go fuzzy and I knew that I had to get out of there. I went for a walk and as I did Dean followed me out and came with me. He just asked if I was ok and listened to what I had to say. I needed to get out and get some air. I was only gone for a short while, when I came into the room again the feeling came back in my head, although not as bad. We contacted the midwife and she said that she would now go and get our baby. Everyone decided to go into the other room and let me and Sophie have time with him first then they would come see him afterwards. We were on our own for about twenty Minutes before we decided that we should name him and as I have the same name as my dad I have always said that my first born son will be named after us. I also wanted Rob's name to be with him as well so we decided to call him David Robert Tomkins-Place we double barrelled his name because Sophie and I are not married. Soon after we had named baby David I remember feeling sick and my head was still feeling like it was going to explode, I kept holding Sophie's hand and I started shaking, I had no idea what baby David was going to look like. I was so worried that he would look dead and that image would stay with me forever and that would be the worst thing for me. My heart was beating so fast then I heard the door handle click open and my heart just melted, As soon as I saw baby David lying in the mosses basket looking like he was just peacefully sleeping. I hugged Sophie and all my bad feelings just washed away. My head cleared instantly, it was the weirdest feeling that I have ever felt in my life, and I could not believe that at 11:00 a.m. I was going round to see Sophie because I thought that she was ill and then at around 8:00 p.m. I was sat looking at my baby boy. He looked beautiful the midwife had dressed him in a stripy yellow and white baby suite and wrapped him in a blue and white blanket. When Sophie was holding Baby David I felt so angry that she was not going to get the chance to feed him and bath him or even change him, I was angry that I would never get the chance to take him to his first football match or even take him to play his first football game. I could feel the anger building up, then Sophie past him over and all that disappeared as I held my baby boy in my arms, nothing else in the world mattered at that moment. This was Sophie, Baby David's and my time and I felt the proudest I have ever felt in my life even through all my pain. Looking back on it now it is weird having all of them emotions in a matter of minutes. Our families were great they did not want to overpower us with lots of people coming to see him at once so they decided that Sophie's family would come in and meet him first. I handed Sophie Baby David and we let the Midwife know that we were ready for the family to come in. Sophie and I hardly had any tears when we first met baby David, but as soon as Angie, Rob, Jim and Matt came in that was it, the tears were flowing out fast and furiously. It was a strange feeling for me because they all kept apologising and I remember thinking that it was me that should be apologising, because I blamed myself for bringing all this pain to them. I felt like I had robbed them of their happiness of their first grandchild so again another emotion was going through my head. But once again I looked down at our little angle and all these thoughts disappeared. Once Sophie's family had been and gone my family came in and I burst into tears. I remember looking into my dad's eyes and seeing the pain then seeing my mum and I did not think that I could cope, then Sophie just took my hand and I knew that I had to stay strong for her and everyone else. Once both families had spent some time with us they returned back to the family room for me and Sophie to have some time alone again. They all came back just before the chaplain came to do the blessing and we tried to tell everyone what his name was, me and Sophie had gone through it about twenty times and were fine but every time we went to tell the family nothing would come out. Sophie tried first then she got all choked up and I went to say it and I just could not get the words out of my mouth. I remember looking up and everyone looking at me with anticipation as if to say well spit it out. In a mixed up blubbering mess Sophie and I said one name each. I did not know how the family was going to react to the news but luckily they accepted it. The chaplain came into our room and we had a little blessing service for baby David, we felt we needed to do this to give him his name. It was about 10 o'clock now both families decided that it was time they left so that we could try and get some rest the hospital were brilliant and let me stay with Sophie. They said their goodbyes to baby David and left. The midwife said that we could keep baby David over night with us if we wanted to. At first Sophie and I said yes, but at about 2 o'clock we were both getting tired everything had calmed down now and we both were just sat holding our son on the bed. The midwife that had been looking after us all day had to clock off, so a second midwife came and met us and asked if we wanted to have some pictures taken with baby David because they were going to make us a memory box. After we had the photos taken we decided that it was best if we did not have Baby David over night but that we were going to see him one last time in the morning. We could see changes in him as time was going on but this was our decision. Sophie and I lay together talking about random things it was weird because at one point we would be laughing about something then crying then silent, just as we had previously throughout the day. I remember asking her what songs we should have at his funeral and I sat singing all different types of songs. They sounded really bad at times and we joked that the midwife would be sitting outside the room at the desk saying "I hope they fall asleep soon."It was about 4 o'clock when I first dropped off Sophie had already fallen asleep I remember just laying their looking at her thinking how brave she had been today and feeling all this love for her. I then woke up at around 6 o'clock and Sophie was having a check over by the midwife to make sure she was ok and checking what she wanted for breakfast. So Sophie and I sat up talking about lots of rubbish now we were both wide awake. We then started to discuss whether we did actually want to see baby David again, because when we saw him last night he looked so peaceful and we knew that nature would have started to take its toll on his little body. Mum phoned me at about half past seven and said that we should seriously consider not seeing baby David again. We discussed it further and decided that last night with our son was precious to us and that we did not want our last memory of our beautiful son to be a bad one. The memories from last night were good ones, where our lovely baby just looked like he was sleeping peacefully. This was the hardest decision we had to make, one other factor that we took into consideration was if we saw him today then we would expect to see him the next day and the next day and so we came to a decision not to see him again. Mum came to the hospital at around 8 o'clock and shortly after she had arrived Angie who had come a few minutes earlier had to leave to go to work. Dean then arrived bringing with him some out of date biscuits and muffin cakes, so we sat comfort eating, the midwives said that Sophie should be able to go home today but we needed to wait for her blood test to come back because she may need an injection. We waited and waited and to pass some time away Dean helped us to pick some possible songs for the funeral.

Finally at around 5 o'clock they came in and said that she did need an injection. She had the injection then the midwife brought out a box and in there they had got a little bit of baby David's hair, his bracelets, the photos that they took, his hand and foot prints and a card with his weight, height, time of birth and another card with all the details of the blessing. They also gave us the blanket that our son was wrapped in and this gave us great comfort for the next coming weeks because it still had his smell on it. Mum helped herself to the towel that he had been wrapped in immediately after his birth. When we were leaving the hospital it was the hardest thing to do, because Sophie was really upset and I had no idea how I was going to help her. I knew that I had to stay strong for her and the sort of person that I am I could hold my feelings back in order to help Sophie. I also knew that if ever I was feeling sad, angry or upset, I could tell Sophie and she would help me even though she had been through a hell of a lot more than I had. When we got outside Sophie just broke down because we should have had him with us. I was starting to get a bit choked up but I just grabbed Sophie, took a deep breath and we left together.

Chapter 3
Baby David's funeral

Sophie and David and the rest of the family were all up very early, even though it had been very late when everyone had finally gone to bed. Minds had been working overtime throughout the night and no one got much sleep. Luckily the weather was kind; there was a gentle breeze with some clouds and sunny intervals, although there was still a chill in the air. Tina had been working all morning preparing the buffet as close family were meeting at the lodge before the funeral, to have a bite to eat as this was going to be a long day for everyone. Dave, Tina's husband had been digging holes in the garden ready for Sophie and David, him and Tina, Angie and Robert and Aunties and Uncles to plant a rose bush in memory of Baby David. Matt and two of David's friends arrived to pick up the gas canister, to take it up to the crematorium David's sister, Emma and Neil arrived with Richard. Dean and Michaela arrived next and then Carl and Rachel. Sophie's nana and granddad from her mother's side arrived, with her parents, Angie and Robert and brothers' Jim and Matt. They all planted the rose bush in the holes already dug out in front of Sophie and David. Her uncle Gary and Aunty Karen arrived and everyone began to chat with each other whilst eating the buffet. The atmosphere was sombre. Everyone was still in shock about the whole situation. Some people were just hearing the story for the first time. Soon it was time for little baby David to arrive. His little tiny white casket looked so small amongst the vast amount of flowers surrounding it. The top of the casket and all four sides had a beautiful picture of a head of a lion on it. David has the same tattoo on his arm of the lion which he had done after his granddad died. The casket also had words inscribed on it that Dean had written for baby David. They said *'Never given the chance, but forever in our hearts. Rest in Peace.* David took hold of Sophie's hand and led her towards their little baby's casket and together they stood in silence. Tears running down both of their faces, they stood with their heads down, Sophie shaking uncontrollably. Tina and Dave, Angie and Rob walked over together followed by all other family members, each paying their own respect silently. Emma took a few photographs of the flowers for David and Sophie to put into their memory box. It was at this moment that the reality of what had happened hit Michaela and it was written all over her face as she stood watching everyone go up to look at the casket and flowers. She started to weep as she stood looking at the grief Sophie and David were going through and felt very sad at the thought that this was the first meeting she had had with baby David, the only memory she will ever have of him. Sophie, David, Angie, Robert, Dave and Tina got into the car that was to follow the Hurst. Everyone else got into their own cars. As the funeral possession pulled out of the park and made its way towards the big cast iron gates at the entrance, Tina noticed the park keeper, his wife and other neighbours all standing there with their heads bowed as a mark of respect. This brought a huge lump to her throat. The possession had to all get through the traffic lights which only let three cars at any one time through, so the possession had to pull into a lay-by and wait for the others to get through. Everyone travelled together to the crematorium. As it came into sight, Sophie and David became overwhelmed at how many people had turned out to support them through this traumatic day. Friends from college, friends from Drama school and even friends of their parents had turned up. The Hurst pulled up outside the south chapel and came to a stop. Andy and Debbie opened the car doors to let everyone out of the car. Sophie and David walked towards the Hurst and stood there for a few moments. Then Andy lifted baby David's tiny casket up and gave it very carefully to Sophie and David to carry together to his resting place. As they looked towards their family and friends they could see there was not a dry eye to be seen. David placed one of his arms around Sophie's back and held onto her tightly, whilst trying to take as much of the weight as he could of their little angels casket, as he was aware Sophie was so desperately trying to hold herself together. She could no longer stop her whole body from shaking. The tears began to flow like a river down her face and it was plain for all to see the pain they both had to endure at that precise moment. The entry music 'The calling- Wherever you will go' began to play. They started to slowly walk down the chapel carefully cradling Baby David's casket, knowing that each step they took was a step closer to saying their goodbyes to their beautiful baby son. The seats in the chapel soon filled up; at the front were Sophie, David, Tina and Dave. Behind them sat Angie, Robert, Jim and Matt. Robert began to sob uncontrollably. He was feeling it for his only daughter and grieving so badly for his grandson. Andy began carefully placing people along the sides of the chapel, so that everyone could see and hear the service. Dean heard one of the songs being played that he had helped David and Sophie pick whilst at the hospital with them as the words were so meaningful and fitting for the service. He recalls looking at them both as they carried baby David's tiny white casket together. Sophie was there holding tightly to David with one hand and the other holding onto the casket. He did not know how they were going to get through the service.

Andy started the service by welcoming everyone to baby David's special service and how he had felt privilege to be asked to do the service. He explained it was close to his heart as he too had suffered the pain of losing his daughter who was still born some 5 years earlier, so he could share the pain that both Sophie and David were feeling. He thanked everyone for being there to support them and after his opening speech, he asked Tina to come up and read the poem her son Carl had written for David and Sophie. Tina's heart began to thump hard against her chest. She thought there was going to be another reading before she had to get up and therefore would have more time to prepare herself and steady her nerves. She squeezed her husband's hand and as she walked past David and Sophie she put her hand on both of their shoulders. As she got to the platform she glanced up at everyone as they waited to hear the poem. She knew her son was going to get up to try to read what he had written for the service and so she had to show it could be done. The poem went as follows:

A Life cannot be measured
In any amount of time
It is measured in people you have touched
In their Heart and in their mind

You will always be remembered
While you look down at us from above
And until we are reunited
We send you all our love

So you go now to the Heavens
But in our hearts you will remain

And we will think of you every day
Until we meet again

Although Tina was shaking badly from head to toe, she managed to say the whole poem only pausing once to steady her nerves. She did not bother to look at anyone before returning back to her seat. The chapel was silent apart from the occasional noise from people who were crying. Andy addressed the people at the service and talked to them about the shock the family got when baby David arrived suddenly without anyone's knowledge of him being there and the wonderful support both families had shown and how they had come together in such a short time to help David and Sophie, as best they could in this terrible tragic situation that had been thrust upon them at such a young age. Once he had delivered his speech music was played to give everyone a moment to sit quietly and reflect. The music was 'Trinity – Fields of Gold.' Andy sat down himself whilst this was playing and then when it had finished he stood back up to read out a family thought that Angie had spent time putting together. Angie had known she would not be able to read out the family thoughts on the day of the service, as it would all be too overwhelming by the time it came to read it. So Andy had agreed he would stand up and read it for her. It was called 'Dear Baby David' and read as follows:

Dear baby David,

I wanted to reflect on your maternal family and how we are feeling about you.

I think as a family we are perhaps a little bit mad, or eccentric, but then I guess so are most families. I think we consist of lots of unique characters who are very different but very close. Your immediate family consists of me, your Nan Angie, your granddad Robert, your Uncles James and Matthew, last but not least your darling mum Sophie. And your dad David who has become so very special to us, You have great grandparents Lillian and Ron , Linda and Bob, great auntie's and uncles and lots of 2nd cousins'

As a family we are able to show each other an abundance of love and support, through happy and sad times we all know we are there for each other, we have shared the hard times with tears and laughter, and our love and acceptance of each other. We all love animals and they are all eccentric too, it just adds to the character of us I think.

You came as a surprise to us all totally unannounced and unexpected, it was chosen that you not stay with us and we confess that leaves our hearts truly broken, As a family we would have easily adapted and accepted your appearance, it might have been untimely not planned but that so didn't matter, given the chance we would have all loved to love you, teach you, cuddle you, play with you, tease you, chase you, tickle you, just amble along with you at our side. You would have been fed a staple diet of love, food and football, compulsory I'm afraid if you are a Tomkins or a Place. Bless you; you would definitely have had a blue kit, but Pompey or Chelsea that would be the question? I am sure you would have been a perfect little diplomat.

The hospital said that they couldn't believe what a lovely family you had, and how lovely it was to see two families come together in support of each other. I can see that your Dad's family mirror ours; lots of characters who together form a lovely family, providing love and support for each other, we know your other grandparents Tina and Dave your aunties Emma, Michaela and Rachel, your uncles Richard, Dean and Carl and your only cousin Ella are hurting and aching as we are.

We all didn't know how you could desperately miss something so badly that we never knew we had. We held your perfect little being in our arms for such a short time and our hearts are filled we pain, because your visit was so fleeting. All we can ask is that you are loved in heaven; you were obviously far too precious for this world. You have touched our hearts and will remain there forever in our thoughts

Bless you darling David Robert Tomkins-Place

Andy then turned to David and asked if he was ready and able to approach his friends and family. David looked at Sophie bent over and gave her a tender kiss on her cheek and then took up his position ready to deliver his speech. Everyone was silent as they watched in anticipation for David to begin. Tina moved near Sophie to comfort her. Dean could not get over how his youngest brother had battled through his emotions and manage to stand up in front of all his friends and family and read out all what he wanted to say at the service. Dean was pleased he had Michaela at his side, as he recalls the last time he ever felt this upset was at his granddads funeral. Michaela could not see much throughout the service as her tears fell freely the whole way through. She remembers holding tightly onto her tiny bump. She just kept looking towards David and Sophie and then at the little white casket placed at the front of the chapel alongside them both. She felt apprehensive for David as he stood at the front trying to compose himself before starting his speech. David bent over close to the microphone bowed his head and then swore. He promptly apologised as he realised it had been heard by everyone at the service. This was the David we all knew always creating a lighter atmosphere for the people watching him. As he spoke his voice broke on a number of occasions and there were times he had to stop and pull himself together, but everyone realised just how hard and painful this was for a young lad who had had to grow up overnight and become the tower of strength for not only himself but for that of his girlfriend as well. His speech was as follows:

Can I take this opportunity to thank everyone for coming, Sophie and I wouldn't have been able to get through this, if it wasn't for the fantastic support of all our family and friends, so thank you and we love you all.

I don't really know what to say as Baby David was a shock to both Sophie and I, when he sprung upon us. That day was such a whirl wind of emotions to find out we were going to be parents and feeling the most proudest we have ever felt. To then have it snatched away from us in a second, I know it ripped a massive hole in both our hearts, we were lucky enough to have been able to spend a few precious hours with our son and also introduce him to our wonderful but sometimes mental families. We were also given the opportunity to name and bless baby David with the comfort and support of our families around us, these moments will be cherished and remembered for the rest of our lives. This combined with the memory box put together by the wonderful midwifes who looked after Sophie, baby David and I we feel will help us keep the memory of baby David in our family and also bring us some comfort when we are feeling low.

David paused for a few moments and then finished off his speech with the following:

I would like to read this poem which I'm sure you will all agree sums up our emotions it is called "They say there is a reason"

> *They say there is a reason,*
> *They say that time will heal,*
> *But neither time nor reason,*
> *Will change the way we feel,*
> *For no-one knows the heartache,*
> *That lies behind our smiles,*
> *No-one knows how many times we have broken*
> *down and cried,*
> *We want to tell you something,*
> *So there won't be any doubt,*
> *You're so wonderful to think of,*
> *But so hard to live without.*

I'm thankful to Baby David, because if there is one thing that he has done for me and I'm sure Sophie too is that he has helped me grow in life from a boy to a man and also bring me and his mum closer together and unite two families. So thank you Baby David we love you with all our

hearts and you will always remain our sleeping little angel.

You could have heard a pin drop; absolutely every single person attending the service was in tears. Andy broke the silence by telling everyone he was now going to do the commendation. Sophie and David together gently picked up Baby David's casket and carried it for the very last time to the platform. Putting it down carefully and placing their hands on top of the casket they both sobbed their young innocent hearts out. Andy stood close to them and repeatedly asked them if they were okay. He said the commendation prayer as he too placed his hand on top of the casket. Then he invited the family to come up and place their yellow roses on top of the casket and say their final farewells to Baby David Robert Tomkins-Place and then he invited everyone to the garden of remembrance to release the balloons. Whilst 'Oasis – Let there be love' played. One by one the family members approached the casket and those who had a yellow rose, placed them on top of it. Some kissed their hands and placed it on the casket others just placed their hands on it, but one by one they all fell apart, before making their way out of the chapel to where the flowers had been placed. After taking a moment to look at them and read some of the beautiful words written on the cards they made their way to the gardens. They were all given a blue balloon to hold onto and then waited for Sophie and David to come. Andy said a few words and then read the following poem:

An angel never dies
Don't let them say I wasn't born,
that something stopped my heart,
I felt each tender squeeze you gave,
I've loved you from the start.

Although my body you can't have,
it doesn't mean I'm gone,
this world was worthy not of me,
God chose that I move on.

I know the pain that drowns your soul,
what you are forced to face,
you have my word ill fill your arms,
some day we will embrace.

You'll hear that it was meant to be,
God doesn't make mistakes,
but that won't soften your worst blow
or make your heart not ache.

I'm watching over all you do,
another child you'll bear,
believe me when I say to you that I am always there.

There will come a time I promise you,

when you will hold my hand,
stroke my face and kiss my head,
and then you will understand.

Although I've never breathed your air,
or gazed into your eyes,
that doesn't mean I never was,
an angel never dies.

Andy once again said more comforting words: **'An angel from the book of life wrote down my baby's birth and whispered as she closed the book too beautiful for earth.'** Then he started to play 'Eric Clapton-Tears in Heaven.' Half way through the song David and Sophie released their balloons and then everyone released theirs. It was the most beautiful, uplifting feeling that you could ever wish to feel under the circumstances. For a while everyone's head was tilted up to the sky watching the balloons get smaller and smaller until they finally disappeared altogether. One balloon had gotten caught up in the tree and as soon as all the balloons passed it, it seemed to get free and follow. Friends and family gave their condolences to Sophie and David. Some managed to speak to them others just wiped their eyes and shook their heads as they struggled to hold their feelings together. They had all been invited back to the 'The British Queen' public house to celebrate Baby David's short life. Everyone at the funeral commended David and Sophie for the dignified way that they had held themselves together at the service. No one was more proud of them than their immediate families. They all agreed the service was well thought out and beautifully put together and a very fitting way for a send off for Baby David.

Sophie and David could not believe how many people came back to the pub to share their love for Baby David. At first the mood was heavy, Sophie and David went round everyone that was there and thanked them for coming and spoke to them for a short while. A very good friend of Richard's called Lee; had been particularly bad at the funeral and at the wake. He eventually spoke with Tina and explained that 13 years ago he and his partner had experienced a still born child and he had never spoken about her. He never knew if it was the right thing to do and so had suffered in silence all those years. Today was the first time he had felt he could talk about his loss and release his hidden grief. In a strange way seeing the way we all dealt with the situation, made him think differently about it. As the night went on the mood lifted and tears turned to laughter. Two hours into the wake, David got everyone in the pub to get a glass of port and they all toasted Baby David. By the end of the evening everyone that left the pub did so much happier than they were when they first walked in. Sophie and David although quite drunk, did not want the night to end, so they went with a few of their friends onto a club.

Chapter 4

The next morning Tina and Rachel got up early and went to the crematorium to pick up all the flowers, as Sophie and David both felt that there was far too many lovely flowers that people had spent a lot of money on, to just let them wither away. There was not one corner of the car that was not covered with flowers and they had to be juggled around a few times to get them all in. They were all placed on one of the decking areas at the lodge. Photographs were taken before some of the flowers were given to family members to take home. Some were taken to a day centre and some were given to friends. The rest were left on the Decking area for all to see whenever they wanted to. Ella, David's niece had wanted to attend the funeral, however as she was so young it was decided that it would be too upsetting for her to see this. Ella had been told that baby David had just not woken up when he was born as he was poorly, because she would see the photographs of him and no one wanted her to know these were photographs of baby David when he was dead. Ella constantly asked questions about baby David and told Sophie on a number of occasions about how she can see his star most nights shining brightly in the sky. She was told about the balloons that were set free after the funeral and she had been allowed to see this part of the DVD that had been taken of the funeral service. Michaela had thought it would be a good idea for Sophie, David, Ella, Dean, Tina, Dave, Angie, Rob and herself to have a little ceremony for Ella where they could set off some Chinese lanterns for baby David. So everyone met at the lodge to do this. Unfortunately, it did not go according to plan as the wind was a little too strong. The first one caught fire before it took off. The second one blew across a tree and onto a bench and David had to run round to it to put it out before it caused any damage. It was a bit of a disaster but everyone managed to see the funny side of things. Ella's granddad Dave had been given a '5' and a '7' balloon for his birthday which was about 2ft in height, she had been promised that a few days after his birthday she could release them into the sky for baby David. She tied a yellow rose to the bottom of the string on both balloons and then let them go. As it was a clear day she could see them for a while getting higher and higher into the sky before disappearing out of view. Ella managed to get a lot of comfort from doing this and constantly talked about baby David being her cousin. One day on visiting, Ella showed her nana Tina and Sophie a picture she had drawn and put on her wall. It was a picture of Baby David's casket with a cross on it, with flowers all the way round it and family members and Tina's dog 'Alfie' standing round. At first it seemed a strange picture for a child to draw, but Ella had put a lot of thought and effort into the picture and it was felt it was her way of dealing with the sadness.

It was a trying time for both Sophie and David, for each day that past Sophie became more and more upset and talked about trying to have another baby. Things became harder for Sophie and she found it hard to cope with Michaela being pregnant. Sophie was beginning to struggle more and more and tried to find someone that could help her with her grief, but she could not find anyone to help. Tina had developed a bad foot and could hardly put her heal to the floor; it had gotten so bad that she went to the doctors about it and whilst she was there she broke down in front of the doctor. Tina decided one day to walk along the sea wall by where she lived, with her dog Alfie. The tied was in and she could hear the waves bashing against the wall, so she sat for a while gathering her thoughts. She felt a hand on her shoulder and when she turned around there was a nun sitting next to her. She was very softly spoken and before long Tina was talking to her about her grandson and all that had just happened. The nun had seen the flowers as she had walked by the lodge and so came back with Tina for a drink and a chat. It helped to have someone who was not connected to the family listen to her and she began her healing process. Sophie was still struggling with her emotions and each night she was having terrible nightmares. David had grown black rings around his eyes as he was not sleeping, because he was aware Sophie was having bad dreams that was waking her up and unsettling her through the night. He wanted to be there for her as much as was humanly possible, night or day. They were both in a vicious circle. David wanted to be there to support the woman he loved and Sophie wanted to be there for the man she loved and neither of them was grieving properly because of this. Sophie tried everywhere to get someone to help them through the grief, but there was just nothing or no one out there to help. Angie and Tina gave as much of their time as they could to just talk over events with Sophie, but quite often it would end up with all three of them crying as the grief was so bad and still raw for everyone. Tina knew that David was suffering in silence. He was very short tempered and not enjoying his football. David's emotions were playing havoc with him and it was plain for all to see. There would always be hurdles that that would come along that they would have to face and it was not long before the first one approached. Sophie had to face 'Mother's Day'. Angie and Tina had decided it would not be appropriate this year to celebrate it, so all the family went out for a meal together just to mark the occasion and then let it go without a fuss. Shortly after this date it was David's birthday and once again no one was in the mood to celebrate, so the families decided to just mark the occasion by meeting at a restaurant and after the meal they all went to the pub owned by David's parents and have a few drinks together before returning home later that evening.

Sophie had decided it would be too hard to go back to her part time job, but felt it might be time to return to college. David dropped her off at the building where she was studying and then went off to the drama section of the college he was studying in. David had been back a few times, but was finding it hard today, as he knew Sophie was really struggling being back at college. Her friends were very good with her. She found some people on the course chose to ignore her rather than have to talk about her losing her baby. Others decided to try and treat her as they always had. But it took just one person to knock her off her feet and that is exactly what happened when she was in the corridor going to the canteen to get something to eat and meet David. The girl to be fair would not have known what she had gone through, she saw Sophie carrying the teddy in her arms and made fun of her for it. Sophie was so upset that she could not pluck up the courage to explain why she was holding onto the teddy so tightly. Instead she put her head down and tried desperately to find David so he could take her home. This one incident knocked her confidence back so far that Sophie had to study at home as she could not face college after this. There were times Sophie was beginning to think she was the only one grieving for her child and that people were now moving on with their lives and so she began to get paranoid that they were starting to forget her lovely son.

Michaela was getting bigger and the baby was kicking a lot. On one occasion when she was visiting with Dean, everyone was talking about her unborn son and Tina could see Sophie was struggling and yet trying hard not to show it. No one else seemed to be aware of this happening. The baby kicked and David without thinking put his hand on Michaela's stomach to feel the kick. Sophie was horrified and shocked at David for doing this and Tina immediately picked up on the hurt she was feeling, so she tried to change the subject quickly and rolled her eyes at David towards Sophie, so he would pick up on how Sophie was feeling. He went straight over to Sophie to give her a reassuring cuddle, it was not until after Dean and Michaela had left that Tina mentioned how hurtful it had been for his girlfriend to witness him feeling another unborn child kick. Sophie had never experienced her son kicking as she had not had any idea she was pregnant. David was horrified when he realised just how hurt Sophie had felt. Tina had heard of a clairvoyant lady who had given a good message to one of her friends and so she had booked a reading for her and Sophie. When they arrived at the woman's house, she was just going out with her dog. She told Sophie and Tina that someone had cancelled the appointment. No one could understand this at all and so the woman decided to let them have the reading. Tina and Sophie sat together in the kitchen. Sophie had hidden the teddy inside her bag from the woman. She told Sophie about the loss of a child and also told her at the end of the reading about a teddy that was supposed to have been placed in the casket and yet she had kept it and placed a much smaller one there instead. She was also told she would eventually have children and the next one would be a girl, but it would not happen straight away as Sophie needed to give her body and her mind time to heal. Sophie left the woman's house feeling a little better than she did before she went in. She told Tina that although it was nice to know her baby was being cared for by other members of her family that had passed over, she wanted to be caring for him and she wanted to have been given the chance to be a mummy to him. Sophie and Tina talked all the way home. Angie was impressed when Sophie told her about the reading she had just had, so much so that she too decided to have a reading herself.

As time passed by Sophie was not managing to get her head above water and she was still struggling with her feelings and her guilt. Sophie and her mother Angie had started weight watchers again and also were now attending Zumba classes with Tina. Sophie could see her weight spiralling out of control and it was not for what she was eating. This was adding to her depression and to top it all off, she now was nearing her final exams at college. Everything seemed to be falling in on top of Sophie and she was sinking further and further into a black hole. Angie knew she was going to have to try and get help for her grieving daughter and so had to go down the road of paying for a private councillor. Angie too was not feeling like she was getting through the grief of losing her first grandchild and so she too decided she should have counselling to help her and then she would be hopefully strong enough to support her daughter. It was not something that could be sorted out overnight but there was just far too much for Sophie to cope with herself. She felt she had not done very well at all with her exams after struggling to get to college to take them. She could not decide what she wanted to do with her life now and her mother felt it may be better for her to try and find a job to take her mind off things. Sophie had mixed feelings as she did not feel strong enough mentally to cope with work and yet sitting around all day was allowing her mind to constantly go over the death of her beautiful baby. Sophie's contact with her friends had now become less and less and this too was having an effect on Sophie. People see it all the time, when someone suffers the loss of a close relative after the funeral is over they do not see much of their friends and they feel people avoid them for fear of not knowing what to say to them. David was now focusing a lot of his energy on finishing his three year national diploma course in drama at college and still trying to spend as much time as he could with Sophie. They had been offered to take time out and go to Majorca where Sophie's grandparents lived for a week. Angie also decided to accompany David and Sophie to try and overcome the terrible feelings she was still trying to cope with. David had a dilemma, he had a show that he had an important part in and it meant he would have to return home the day before Sophie and her mother. At first because of this show he had decided not to go as he had lines to learn and rehearsals. But after discussing it with his mum and Sophie about how they had not had any time away from each other since the death of their baby and the fact they needed to take some time out to grieve properly he eventually changed his mind. This was probably one of the best decisions he made, because when the holiday finally arrived he realised he would not have wanted the week away from Sophie.

Sophie's dad took them off to the airport and David let his parents know when they had arrived in Majorca. This meant that Dave and Tina could also relax a while whilst their son was away from home, being cared for by Sophie's mother and grandparents. David had taken his script away with him to make sure he knew his lines ready for when he returned home. Once the week was over David's parents were at the airport to pick their son up and were pleased to see he was looking better for having had the holiday. They knew that this was going to be a testing time for him having to spend the first night apart from Sophie. Surprisingly David did manage to sleep well that evening and Tina knew her son was finally coming to terms with his loss and starting to move his life forward a little at a time. Sophie returned the next evening and she too looked well on the short break away. She had tanned up in the week, which gave her a nice glow. David managed to get through his performance, watched by Sophie, Tina and Ella. It was a good laugh and had been a tonic for her and Sophie. Sophie was at this time still carrying teddy around with her everywhere.

David's father had booked a week away for a golfing holiday and so his aunty Les had been brought to Portsmouth as a surprise for his mother. Whilst she was here for the week they decided to sit down with her and watch the DVD of the funeral. She had not been able to attend the funeral and so a special time was set aside. It was very hard to watch but it opened a topic of conversation which lasted all day after watching the service. There were a lot of tears shared by everyone but it was something that they thought they would not be able to do. Sophie and David both agreed that there was a lot of the service which had been a total blank to them and watching the DVD filled in a lot of the gaps. Having Les down was good for Tina as she is a good listener and good at giving advice. It may not always be what you want to hear but you could be sure, it would be good advice. There were evenings that Tina and Les would let their hair down and then there would be evenings where they would sit out on the decking and just chat the night away with the help of a few drinks. This week had been good for Tina and in some respects good for Sophie and David. Dave had been able to take his mind of the pressures of the past few months with his fellow golf mates and so individually this had helped everyone. A few weeks after Les went home, Sophie and David attended an appointment at the hospital to talk over with the consultant what they believed had caused the death of baby David. They were told that Sophie had produced a blood clot, which had eventually burst in her womb which caused the death of her baby. He went on to say that she had a 1 in 5 chance of this happening again and if she chose to get pregnant again, they would make sure she was monitored regularly, to try to prevent this ever happening again. The stats seemed extremely high and although it answered questions for both of them, it did not seem to make any difference to how Sophie was feeling.

David and Sophie had been thinking about having a tattoo done to remember their baby son and after many discussions about it, David's brothers started to discuss what tattoo they could have done as well. Over the next few weeks there was a lot of planning and discussions about the tattoos until eventually they were all happy with their choice. David had chosen a tattoo of an angel holding a baby in her arms and her wings surrounded the whole picture. He was having this done on his back between his shoulder blades. Sophie was having a beautiful butterfly which she associates with her baby boy, on her back above her left shoulder. Dean was having hands praying with rosary beads hanging over the hands and the words *"David Robert Tomkins-place my brave nephew never given a chance but forever in our hearts. Born and died 23rd February2011"* Richard had the words *"and maybe I'll find out a way to make it back to you. To watch you, to guide you through the darkest of your days. If a great wave shall fall upon all then I hope there is someone out there who can bring me back to you"* on his stomach. Carl does not like tattoos and so did not have one done. They all had these tattoos done on the same day and Tina and Michaela went with them to watch their faces as they had them done one by one. She worried about Dean having his as he has a phobia of needles and just could not imagine him having this done, especially because of the size of it. However, although it took a whole day each one of them braved it. David's was a lot bigger than anyone imagined and it was quite obvious to everyone, how painful it was for him to have this done. He said that Sophie had endured a lot of pain when she gave birth to their son and so he would cope with this pain. Even when the tears were streaming down his face and he could not clench his teeth anymore he held on until it was completely finished. He could have had more white put onto the wings of the angel, but he just could not cope with it anymore. Dean had now started a new job and Carl had moved back down south to be closer to his family and had moved back into the flat above the pub, where Richard lived too. Carl had been successful in getting a job at the same place as Dean. Time was getting closer for the arrival of Dean and Michaela's baby. There had been complications and she had been told she would need a c section as her baby was breach and showed no signs of turning. Dean and Michaela had found a new house to move into as the one they lived in was only two bedrooms and they now wanted three bedrooms. Their new house also has a lot more space downstairs. Sophie, David, Tina and Dean's friends Rich and Pete helped him move. Many items had been moved prior to the removal date and so the move went really smoothly, which is a good job as Michaela was only two weeks away from giving birth.

July 20th 2011 Michaela and Dean give birth to their 7lb 9oz baby boy and David, Sophie, Dave and Tina went up together to visit them. Tina picked Ella up from school and after tea they all made their way to the hospital. Tina was worried about how she was going to react when she finally met grandson number two and at the same time was worrying about how Sophie and David were going to cope. Michaela was not in the same ward as Sophie which was a bonus. Tina and Dave took Ella to meet her baby brother; this helped Tina as she had to make sure Ella was okay. As she caught sight of Michaela and Dean through the curtains her eyes lit up and her smile stretched from ear to ear as she snuggled up next to her dad and Michaela. Tina kissed her son Dean and Michaela and told them both she was so proud and so pleased to meet grandson number two. She bent over to where her little grandson was asleep in his crib with beautiful rosy cheeks. He was making a little grunting noise as he took little breaths. She held back her tears and swallowed hard to remove the lump in the back of her throat. Dean took hold of his son and passed him to his granddad Dave to have a cuddle. After Dave had had his cuddles he handed him over to Tina. She tenderly held him in her arms and the memories of her first grandson came flooding back to her. The last baby boy she held in her arms just a few months ago left her with the biggest hole in her heart. This little grandson was warm, soft and had a beautiful healthy colour to him, unlike her first grandson. She remembered the feeling of his lifeless body, cold, rigid and pale as she cradled him in her arms. She kissed her grandson and then gave him back to Dean so that she could go and let David and Sophie come and see the new addition to the family. The hospital would only allow two visitors at a time, so in order for them to come in Dave and Tina had to go out. Tina watched David and Sophie with apprehension as they made their way to the ward where Dean and Michaela were waiting their arrival. Sophie held her breath as she made her way towards them. Dean was sitting with his son in his arms and Michaela was sitting on the bed with Ella. David held onto Sophie's hand tightly and did not let go until they were sitting on the seats next to Dean. David had a cuddle of the new baby first and after having his photo taken with his nephew, he carefully handed him over to Sophie. Sophie's heart was beating hard and her whole body was trembling as she fought to hold her emotions together. Just as Dean had fought his emotions for David and Sophie, they were now doing the same, only this time the tears that followed were tears of joy as this time there was a happy ending. Dean and Michaela had dreaded this day as no one knew how they were going to cope or react to meeting Joey their baby for the first time. Dean was so surprised when they walked into the room where they were waiting with anticipation. There had been moments leading up to the birth when Sophie had been upset, but throughout he felt they had been wonderful giving the circumstances. They showered Joey with lots of gifts in the days after his birth and gave him as many cuddles as they could possibly give him.

Dean and Michaela decided there could only be one choice for godparents and that was David and Sophie. He knew they could never replace their precious son, but Joey would provide a lot of cuddles and kisses for them and help them heal whilst they joined in helping to bring him up. Michaela feels that sometimes David and Sophie look at Joey and see the child they lost in him. Tina looks at grandson number two and wonders all the time what little baby David would look like now. However his arrival has helped more people than he will ever know heal and as little as he is he already has his own little character. Richard bought a Pompey sleep suit for Joey with his name printed on the back of it and when David saw him give it to Dean and Michaela it was plain for all to see the pain and upset it caused him. Richard said to David at the time "welcome to my world" and this brought David back down to earth. There is always going to be some situation that will bring out these upsetting feelings but luckily we have strong families and this is what will help everyone get through.

In August this year David's Uncle Brian, Aunty Lesley and cousin Rian came from Newcastle for a short break. Sophie had not met Brian before, but had heard a lot about him. He was just as crazy as David and when the two of them meet up there is never a dull moment. The week they visited was a tonic for everyone. It was a week packed of laughs and tears, a time when families could get together to share moments about a situation that would leave a mark on everyone's heart forever and then move their lives forward. Brian like David has always been the light hearted family member, full of fun and always living life to the full wherever possible. Les has always kept Brian grounded and the same can be said about Sophie and David. Everyone went out of their way during this week to try and have a time to relax and put some fun back in their lives. We had organised a karaoke in the pub on Saturday 6th August 2011 to wet Dean and Michaela's baby's head. This was a nice family event and god knows we all needed one. Dean and Dave had witnessed a dog drowning and so Brian had dived into the sea to rescue him. The dog had drowned but Brian refused to give up on it and started to try to revive it with the help of Dean and Dave. Somehow the dog survived and everyone was overwhelmed by it. However, through the early hours of the morning tragedy struck again, when the pet dog Alfie, of eleven years became seriously ill and was rushed to the vets. He unfortunately died and this cast a terrible sadness over everyone in the family again. It was yet another painful situation to have to go through. The situation was made somewhat easier by having Brian, Lesley and Rian there. There was so much to sort out as Alfie had left a terrible mess in the new place. Everyone pulled together to help, Brian set to cleaning every carpet in the lodge, whilst Lesley worked her magic and got the place smelling fresh again and Somehow Sophie and David became a tower of strength to Tina to help her deal with the pain of losing her soul mate. Although her pain could be in no way compared to the pain David and Sophie had gone through, it did show that they were capable of both putting their feelings and their pain to one side and try to repay some of the compassion they had received when they needed it most. The power of love that families can give when united is second to none and with both David and Sophie's families uniting this year they have conquered everything thrown their way and started to lift their heads up and move forward once again. It is something that is not going to happen overnight and some will take longer than others to learn to live with the loss of a beautiful baby. What made it all that much harder to cope with was not knowing he was there and that is one of the reasons he is now know as our 'hidden angel' who will live in our hearts for eternity.

Chapter 5

Sophie has gone through counselling and still struggles without her baby. There is not a day goes by when she does not have a quiet moment to reflect on her loss. She still has terrible nightmares which affect her sleep most nights and longs for the day they finally end. She is now at work full time and has finally learned to leave teddy at home. However it is the first thing she looks for when she arrives home and he still sleeps right by her side every night. Although teddy is dirty now, Sophie cannot bring herself to wash him, so he remains as he was the day she bought him. She still has many battles emotionally ahead of her but has just learned to take one day at a time now.

David has never truly shown his emotions and does not really talk to anyone about losing his son. That is until he was asked to put his thoughts down for this book. This was the first time that David has opened up and allowed others to know how he truly felt, by putting his feelings into words for all to read. By doing this he has finally let go of all the emotions he had locked away. Sophie bought David a Pompey sleep suit and hat set with baby David's name printed on it. She had it framed with a photo of baby David and his name and birth date written on and it has been given pride of place in David's bedroom. The memory box is full and is kept in a safe place and together Sophie and David help each other to get through any bad times. They wait with heavy hearts for their first Christmas and baby David's first anniversary, but with the support of their families they will once again find the strength to move forward and continue to remember there hidden angel with pride and love as always.

Tina still has her little photographs of her precious first grandson on her bedside cabinet and kisses them every night and every morning. She has moved on with the help of her grandson number 2, Joey and her lovely granddaughter Ella, who has always had that special place in her heart. She prays that one day Sophie and David will have their own lovely baby to cherish and love when the time is right for them. Until that time she remains there to support David and Sophie as much as she can.

Dave although could not bring himself to go over the events of that terrible day has always remained strong and supportive for everyone. He has always put his own emotions and feelings to one side, to enable him to be the pillar of strength for his family and will remain this way for as long as David and Sophie need him.

Angie always has said that the hardest thing ever has been to watch Sophie and David pick themselves up from such a tragedy. The saying you can't miss it if you have never had it is not true. She didn't know baby David was coming, she never knew him, but she misses him every day and wished it could have been different. Seeing her daughter in absolute despair and agony has ripped her heart out. Angie thinks she would always fix things for her kids, but for this there has been little she could do. As a mother Angie has battled with the guilt, why didn't she know? Why didn't she go home after ringing her daughter and finding out she was still poorly? She could go on forever with the why's and wherefores, but she just has to accept that it was as it was, and that cannot change. Angie has a picture of David by her bed and he will always be her gorgeous first grandson, bless him, he is forever perfect

Rob will always have that special place in his heart for his precious daughter and no matter how old she gets, she will always remain his little girl. The pain was unbearable for him on that terrible day and again at the funeral. As a father he just wants to be there for both Sophie and David whenever he can, to listen to them, to support them and most of all to protect them.

Dean and Michaela remain as close as ever to David and Sophie and although they were robbed of being parents, they felt honoured and privileged to be asked by Dean and Michaela to be godparents to Joey. Something they will do with pride and commitment and the bond they share will be forever strong. Emma and Neil although have busy lives, never forget to make that important telephone call to keep in touch and show their thoughts are still very much with everyone. Richard, Carl, Jim and Matt go about their normal day to day activities, but Sophie and David know if they ever needed them they just need to ask and they will be there for them.

Lil and Ron showed great empathy during a terrible period and although devastated by it all, kept calm and grounded for Sophie and David. Their love and support has been greatly received by them both and they look forward to their weekly visits, where Lil prepares a full English breakfast to brighten up their day.

Life is far from normal but with the strong love, affection and support we have all received from one another, we are learning to live again.

* 9 7 8 1 9 0 8 7 7 5 4 7 4 *